Wisdom For Life's Journey

Charles H. Ellis III

CHE3 Publishing
PO Box 19357
Detroit, MI 48219

Cover design by Jackie Baptist
Cover photos: Copyright © Istockphoto.com
Page layout by Lee Lewis Walsh, Words Plus Design,
www.wordsplusdesign.com
Editorial assistance by Tenita Johnson,
www.soitiswritten.net

All scripture quotations are from the King James Version
of the Holy Bible.

ISBN 978-0-9708477-8-2

Printed in the United States of America

Acknowledgments

I want to thank God the Creator who is the source of all wisdom, knowledge and understanding. Wisdom is the most principal thing and thanks to Him for so graciously endowing us with His necessary truths for success.

I want to thank my parents, who by their life's examples, instilled many valuable lessons in me which have guided me on my productive journey.

Words cannot express my gratitude to my wife, Crisette Michelle, a phenomenal woman of grace and class for her love, support, and patience throughout our 24 years of marriage.

Thanks to my children Kiera Monet and Charles IV (Buddy) who have taught me so many life lessons that could never be learned except throughout the experiences of parenting.

Lastly, I want to thank my Greater Grace Temple (City of David) family who have stood with me in our ministry effort, and have always expressed their love and support.

Contents

Introduction

There are simple differentiations between success and failure. Define "success" and "failure". The right kind of influence or words of encouragement can be the fuel that empowers your dreams, goals, and aspirations. This inspirational literary piece has been compiled to assist you in reaching your destiny successfully. This book will give you a positive outlook on life. It will inspire you to be secure in who God called you to be. You will be motivated to keep moving toward your destiny by being steadfast and productive along the way.

Each of us has a destiny to fulfill and an appointed time for its manifestation. There are many facets in life that are designed to work against this manifestation. Experience has taught me that the biggest hindrance to our future success is ourselves.

Therefore, it is incumbent upon us to find the proper tools and resources that will cause us to reach our destiny successfully. We alone are responsible for creating and sustaining the fertile environment that will cultivate this kind of success and growth.

This publication has been influenced by my many studies, experiences, and life's realities. Over my life, I have witnessed many great times and some challenging seasons. These times and seasons have caused me to draw on a great reservoir of teachings, words and thoughts to help maintain a positive focus.

I have written this book to speak to you with hope. You will realize the necessary resources to help bring your ordained destiny to fruition. My joy is to know that this writing will resonate with you and give good directions when you need it most.

As you read this book please allow these literary nuggets of wisdom to fortify your determination to have a future of success. Now open your mind, find a quiet place, and get a delicious cup of coffee or juice as you peruse my newest book ... *Wisdom For Life's Journey.*

Wisdom For
Life's Journey

Love Is The Greatest Force

There are great and mighty forces in life that are essential to our survival and good success. Three key forces that come to mind are love, faith and hope, but that which is most key is Love!

Chapter 1

*I*f "love" was an infectious condition that spread throughout the universe, how have you been affected?

Sometimes, it is the will of God that allows circumstances to come in our lives to separate us from others. There are times when it is nothing that you have caused, but it is God working His perfect plan in your destiny.

Do you know that unhealthy relationships are a major cause and distraction of those who are trying to improve their lives and reach their full potential?

I'm certain none of us want to be alone, abandoned, forsaken or alienated from those whom we have grown accustomed to being around and are part of our lives. After all, we have gotten somewhat comfortable with our surrounding of friends, associates, loved ones and lovers.

Oddly enough, we know that many of these relationships are detrimental to our productivity, but we have become complacent in them. Therefore, God sometimes has to do for us, what we are not strong enough to do for ourselves.

Can we be honest? There were often times when I knew that certain people needed to be removed from my life, but I simply couldn't muster up the strength to do it.

I was sadly mistaken to think that having people around meant I was loved. The feeling of emptiness consumed me when the crowd or that "one somebody" had gone.

I have learned over time that true love does not come from others. It comes from God. When you allow love to be dictated by people, then your fulfillment will always be an up and down emotional roller coaster, with many more demoralizing lows than soaring heights.

It was the great writer Rollo May that said, *"The amazing thing about love is that it is the best way to get to know ourselves."* Take consolation in knowing that God is love. He loves you more than you will ever know. When you truly get to know yourself, then you will better yourself, and when you begin to better yourself, it will demonstrate that you now truly love yourself. Suddenly, you have a love that no one can negatively alter or affect.

You are loved today, tomorrow and forever.

The Rewards Of Determination

Determination says that you will be so strong in your mind concerning a matter, that your focus and resolve will be absolute, and nothing will be able to detour you from your goal.

Chapter 2

A story is told about a lady who was determined to arrive at her destination
promptly. She didn't know the route that
would get her there. She asked a kind gentleman,
and he told her to stand at the bus stop and wait
for Bus #10. Later that evening he saw that she
was still standing there and asked why she had
not boarded the bus. She replied that she had
counted nine buses and the next one would be
number 10.

I suggest that you can often consider your
world as being made up of two kinds of people.
There are those who simply wish for things,
thinking that one day they will magically appear.
Others wish for things and are determined to
make them happen.

During my life, I have learned that things
really do not magically appear or come into existence. If you haven't noticed lately, this is not
Kansas and I haven't seen Dorothy in the hood

or suburbs of metropolitan Detroit. The only true effort is hard work and determination. This will bring about the realization of your wishes and goals.

Believing and having faith for your dreams is one thing, but the Bible tells us that *"faith without works is dead."* This spiritual truth says to me that God honors your honest efforts and not just the things that you are able to conjure up in your minds. At some point in time, your body must honor the imagination of your mind if you are truly going to see your dreams become a reality.

There is a very popular saying that goes something like this, *"If you keep doing things the same way then, you will keep on getting the same results"*. Sadly enough, you and I have seen this saying enacted in too many lives over the years. There are so many people with possibilities that are in the wilderness of stagnation. Their promises have become complacent beneath their God-given privilege and calling.

I have always been taught that anything worth having is worth fighting for or struggling to make it happen. Now, when I refer to fighting, I am not necessarily speaking of violence toward others, but rather fighting the enemies of stagnation, complacency, laziness, low self esteem, inferiority, insecurity, weakness and failure. I believe that this is a day and season in which determination has become the *"pivotal key"* to your dreams coming true.

We've often heard that, *"winners never quit and quitters never win."* Allow me to ask this question. Are you a quitter? Does the least and most minute sign of trouble discourage you because you are afraid or too lazy to think critically or analytically? Are you determined, only if you have no opposition or obstacles impeding your progress? Understand that opposition is a part of the real world. Murphy's Law of *what can go wrong will go wrong* sometimes rings true. Many visions and goals will only be realized and accomplished through determination. Quitters should simply prepare themselves for a mediocre, mundane life of unfulfilled dreams, goals and aspirations.

Only those determined to beat the odds, overcome opposition and endure struggles will ever be declared winners. Winners will never quit but they will adjust, refocus and seek another method to reach their destiny. Grab hold of enough faith to believe what God has for you, is for you. Also, be determined not to allow anything to prevent you from receiving what He has planned for your life.

I'm reminded of a scientific study performed a few years ago in one of the Ivy League Universities where a group of scientists endeavored to break the spirit of a frog. As you know, frogs are born with an innate ability to jump and leap. Yet these brilliant, scientific minds set out to change the innate nature of this frog and to diminish its God-ordained abilities and purpose.

Here's what they did: They took this young frog and placed it in a large clear mason jar. They placed a clear top on the jar so that the frog could see above, but of course, he could not jump through the lid. The scientists began to beat upon the jar and naturally the frog began to jump. Yet, every time it would jump, it would hit its head and land back on the bottom. They performed this function for many minutes, hours and days. This frog would continue to jump as they would bang on the jar and it would continually bump its head and land back on the bottom.

After about a week, they broke the spirit of that frog to the extent that as they beat on the jar, the frog would not jump anymore. This frog simply sat in the jar defeated, exhausted and depleted of moral energy. He probably thought to himself, *"there's no use in me jumping because I only hit my head, and fall back down."*

Knowing that the spirit of the frog was broken, the Scientists then took the glass lid off the top of the jar. They placed the jar on a stove and turned the burners on. The fire began to heat the jar, which ultimately made the bottom very hot. Oddly enough, this frog continued to sit on the bottom of this jar and eventually burned to death. Certainly, if only that frog had jumped one more time, he would have been freed from the jar and escaped certain death.

Therefore, in the midst of failed attempts to reach your life's goals, I encourage you to *"jump one more time."* I don't care how disappointed you may be with the cares of life. People may have let you down time and time again, but continue your determination to overcome any odds and impediments coming against you. Pray to God for the tenacity of the bulldog, the persistence of the ant and the determination of the bumblebee! Although scientists claim the bumblebee's body is too heavy for its wings, yet it flies anyway!

A lesson of determination in professional boxing history shows us a young man by the name of Sugar Ray Leonard who was an

Olympic gold medalist, an eventual world champion, and a very wealthy man. What more could this famed sports figure want? Leonard made it clear that he wanted to challenge Marvin Hagler for the middleweight championship. People wondered, "Has Sugar Ray gone mad? Has he lost his mind?" How could a boxer who hadn't fought in five years and nearly lost his vision in one eye, challenge for the middleweight championship?

Marvin Hagler had gone undefeated in the last decade, yet a determined Sugar Ray Leonard said he would be ready. Leonard possessed the determination to prove he was the best middleweight boxer in the world. He initiated a demanding training program, realizing that Hagler was already in tip-top condition. Leonard sacrificed himself for the opportunity to win.

On the night of the fight in Las Vegas, Hagler worked the ring like a charging bull. Leonard danced, pranced and avoided the champion's powerful blows. When it was all said and done, Sugar Ray went home with $11 million dollars and the world middleweight championship belt.

Driven by determination, he defied the odds and the skepticism of boxing fans. The world marveled at Sugar Ray Leonard's comeback to defeat Marvin Hagler. Although he did not land a knock out punch, it was with unshakeable mental focus, physical stamina and an unstoppable determination to win, that he regained his title as middleweight champion of the world.

When you know what you want and you want it badly enough, then you will find ways to get it. Can you be inspired by this thought? *"Be like a postage stamp and stick to something until you get there."*

"Determination" must be unwavering in order to reach your destiny and fulfill His purpose in your lives.

Never Stop Hoping

True hope necessitates a desire for that which has not yet materialized.

Chapter 3

*H*ave you ever considered how many things would never have been established if someone had never grasped the power of hope? Well, I have thought about that on numerous occasions. I look at communities that have been transformed from unseemly blight to pleasant and attractive developments. These transformations are leading the way to a much needed area renaissance.

I am fully persuaded that before you can believe that anything can come to pass, you must first "hope" for such a thing. Someone had to hope for a better community before the first step of renewal was ever taken. Before a foundation was dug, before a pipe was laid, before a brick was fitted into place, someone had to hope.

Think about where you are now and where you are going. How much has your ability to hope contributed to your current position? I can tell you about my life. There has always been a hope that has burned inside of me. A hope that declares, *"It's not over until God says it's over."* As a matter of fact, I am deathly afraid of people that have lost an ability to hope. I consider these the most dangerous people in the world. People with no hope will do anything because they feel, in most cases; there is nothing to look forward to.

I am reminded of one my favorite movies, *"The Shawshank Redemption."* Many of you have seen this blockbuster movie, which is now played over and over again on regular and cable television. Well, there is a scene where the character of Andy (played by Tim Robbins) is conversing with Red (played by Morgan Freeman). Falsely convicted of killing his wife, Andy has been unjustly sentenced to life in prison. Red, on the other hand did the crime, and has been doing the time for so long that he has become institutionalized. Red has been denied parole time after time.

Meanwhile, Andy is in the prison courtyard and looking out at the world dreaming and hoping that one day he will be freed from prison. Red warns him that this kind of hoping can be very dangerous to his sanity. Red tries to get Andy to buy into the fact that his prison term *"is what it is."* and there is nothing he can do about it, nor is there anyone who will plead his case.

Andy has one of two choices: He can either be influenced by Red and accept the unjust sentence or he can keep hoping that some way and somehow, he will be freed by whatever means necessary. Well, not to spoil the ending for those of you who have yet to see this great film, but yes, Andy finds a way to escape prison and live out his life on the ocean shore in Mexico.

He would not allow his hope to die nor be influenced by the hopelessness of others. As a matter of fact, the realization of Andy's hope was so powerful that Red began to hope for his release. After decades of incarceration, he was finally paroled and joined Andy's peaceful, tranquil life in Mexico.

I'm not sure where your thoughts may be concentrated or where your expectations may be. However, it's important to know that you should never allow anybody or anything to cause you to let go of your hope. There is a Bible scripture in the book of Romans that says, *"May the God of hope fill you with all joy and peace as you trust in him, so that you may overflow with hope by the power of the Holy Spirit."* I pray that these inspirational words will inspire you to seek a hope

19

that is not swayed by the disappointments of life and the failures of your past.

Each day is a new day. You must learn to hope in today's possibilities and not be negatively impacted by yesterday's lack of fulfillment. I challenge you to wake up everyday with a new hope for what you desire and look forward to. See every dawning as another chance to realize your aspirations and capture your promise. Again, don't view yesterday as a disappointment but look to today as another chance. After all, who in their right mind doesn't want another chance? Another chance is hope, and hope is not a dangerous thing; but to the contrary, it is a great thing.

How To Handle Storms

You can navigate your way through the greatest storms and dark clouds if you have the right GPS equipment.

Chapter 4

The continuing wake of Hurricane Katrina has caused all of us to consider how we would prepare for and handle storms.

Think about it, almost nothing can bring more fear into one's life than a threatening storm. And in every area of life there are storms (big ones, little ones, brief ones, lengthy, mild, and severe ones). Some are tropical, which you will find in areas where there are great bodies of water. Some are in deserts where sand is blown to high piling levels. Others are on land where boisterous winds can develop into tornadoes, as we've seen over the years in tornado alley, the region of the country where tornadoes are more likely to occur. These storms bring about much damage with staggering losses totaling millions or even billions of dollars. Even worse, hundreds and thousands of lives are lost over time.

Thank God, to our credit today, our society is so technologically advanced until it is very rare that any storm will catch us off-guard. We have perfected all kinds of warning systems to help alert us of pending storms. Our local weather forecasters now have sophisticated radar equipment called *"Doppler"*. This radar can identify, track and measure storms, including their path, velocity and many other relevant factors.

With this science available to us today, it simply makes no sense for us ever to be caught off guard with respect to these potential dangers. As a matter of fact, it is a wise man or woman that will make the necessary preparation for the storms of life that most certainly will come and are on the way.

Let's consider some of the things that we can do to safeguard us against the storms of life:

- Purchase necessary insurances to cover any losses.
- Board up windows and other vulnerable areas.
- Stock up with adequate food supplies (water, can goods, etc).
- Stock up other needful supplies (batteries, generators, fuel).
- Hang on to something that is well anchored.
- Find solace in an adequate storm shelter.

23

- Sometimes it may be necessary to evacuate the area.

These kinds of preparations can prove to be very beneficial during life threatening storms. One can save valuable property and assets that are hard to replace, and preserve life which is certainly irreplaceable.

In the case of Hurricane Katrina, we witnessed those who were prepared and many who were not. Many were negatively impacted and jeopardized for the rest of their lives.

The effects of Hurricane Katrina have not only been natural and physical, but many find themselves suffering mentally, emotionally, and even spiritually. People have lost faith in God because there just seems to be no rationale for this horrific disaster that has plummeted so many people into ruin and devastation.

Some people have unanswered questions like, *"how could God be good and allow something so tragic?"* Others are emotionally drained and appear unable to muster up the energy to bounce back from this adversity. Then, there are those who seem to be in a lethargic mental state and unable to cope with the loss of loved ones, property and valuables.

Thank God for those who have found faith in Him amid this tragedy. They now believe there is an awesome and powerful spiritual force that can take what seems to be evil and turn it around for good. I try not to concentrate on the devastation of Katrina, but rather focus in on the many positive stories that have come out of this event. It's a joy to witness the many people who refuse to surrender to tragedy and adversity, but instead declare that, *"defeat has no place here."*

Katrina has moved many of us to educate ourselves on storms. I have learned that the Atlantic hurricane season alone runs from June 1 through November 30 of each year. Perhaps you were not directly affected by Hurricane Katrina, but you can testify and attest to the reality that there are some figurative storms in your life. After all, the storms of life don't just come in the form of rain and wind.

You may be suffering from one of these varying types of storms.

- Financial storm
- Relationship storm
- Employment storm
- Educational storm
- Health storm
- Spiritual storm

In fact, sometimes it seems as if these storms last even longer than those of the natural hurricane seasons. Maybe you've been robbing Peter to pay Paul for so long until Peter has now turned on you. Maybe you've dealt with so many bad relationships until you can't remember the last time that you felt comfortable in someone's company. Perhaps you've been working for *"temp agencies"* so often until you wonder if permanent employment will ever come your way. Can you remember the last time you felt healthy? Have you lost hope in regaining your well-being?

Well, let me encourage you not to give up, but rather to make the necessary preparations for the storms of life that are sure to come. Nothing beats preparation and a well laid out plan. Remember that someone once said that, *"failing to plan is planning to fail."* We must pray to God each day for the tenacity and perseverance to weather any storm that may come into our lives.

The God of peace will be that anchor that keeps you grounded when the storms of life attempt to blow you away. There certainly is an unshakeable foundation that you can stand on when the storms of life are raging.

The Importance Of A Vision

A person without a vision is a person who will waste away. Life necessitates that we maintain a vision, and always know that every vision has an appointed time.

Chapter 5

There is a scripture in Proverbs 29:18 that says in part, *"Where there is no vision, the people perish..."* What is it that this wise writer is trying to convey to you? What is his message, and why is this suggestion of having a vision so important to your survival? I believe that the composer of the Proverbs was not just speaking of any dream or vision; but more importantly, a vision from God. If indeed God is your Creator, then He must have a purpose for you being created and thereby the necessity of a vision from Him to communicate His will for your lives.

Yes, a vision is absolutely essential to your progress, your productivity, your good success and ultimately your survival. I believe that it was Ms. Helen Keller who once answered when asked, *"is there anything worst than being born blind?"* Her response was, *"yes, I pity those who have their sight, but have no vision."* Does it startle you that a blind person can feel superior to someone who has 20/20 sight? I would like to go on record agreeing with both the writer of Proverbs and Helen Keller that a vision (especially one from God) is more important than all the natural sight in the world and that without such a vision or visions, one is destined to die.

This certain death is not always a physical one, although ultimately it is. It can also be a spiritual death, emotional death, or maybe even a mental death. A vision or visions will power your productivity and progressive state. It is necessary to continue your drive for success while limiting your satisfaction with mediocrity. Throughout history, we can identify many people who credit the power of visions for their success. It is said that Henry Ford (the automotive magnate) failed and went broke five times before his continued vision of cars being assembled on a line brought him unprecedented success. It is also said that James Earl Jones stuttered so badly in school that he was forced to communicate in writing, but his vision of success in the world of fine arts drove him to overcome this impediment and today the rest is history.

Truly, a vision from God can be so powerful that it can overcome anything that dares to pose a threat to it. If you will truly seek a vision and God honors your request, then you will be on a road that leads only to success and fulfillment. God's vision for you will climb any mountain, weather any storm, cross any river, suffer through any desert, march through any valley and outlast any wilderness. A vision from God cannot be stopped. You cannot kill it; you cannot break it; and you cannot destroy it. It is your key to survival and ultimate success. What is your vision? What are your visions? Do you have a vision or visions?

Receiving and grasping hold to a vision or visions is as simple as seeking God's will for your life. Why live day after day with the lack of a vision, stumbling about in mediocrity, complacency and stagnation? Believe me when I say that the absence of a vision will paralyze creativity and where there is no creativity, there can be no productivity, and where there is no productivity there can only be pending death.

God wants you to live a life that is vibrant, abundant, prosperous and filled with potentiality. However, to access this will of His, you must first seek His vision for you. I pray each week for God's vision to come to pass in my life, in my family, in my ministry, and in the lives of our parishioners. I am also thankful to say that time and time again I have seen the visions of God come to pass. How exciting it is to know that God has spoken something or things into your spirit and before you know it; those things are fulfilled right before your eyes.

If you are honest, there is a tendency to come to a prolonged stop and bask in the reward of your completed vision. The danger of this attitude and action is that while you are star-gazing at the fruition of your vision, you can miss the next vision of God. I believe that you can be a person of multiple visions. Once one is completed, there is always another waiting in the wings. Our Lord is a God of progression and productivity. Therefore, you should always be striving for the next vision and move of God.

I encourage you to consider becoming a person of vision. Why not seek a vision or visions? Why should you not have a vision or visions? Why not accept a vision or visions from God? The kinds of visions that come from above are those that believe the impossible, see the invisible, and feel the intangible. Don't settle for mediocrity and live beneath your God-given privilege. Never grow accustomed to stagnation and complacency, rather live life as a true visionary and watch your God-given visions last well beyond your natural existence. Let the God of vision propel you toward a bright and promising future. Where there is no vision, you are sure to perish. Why suffer a slow un-welcomed death when you can live with a vision from God?

The Power Of Your Thoughts

Your thoughts are the launching pads from which your destiny will spring forth. Therefore, guard your thoughts to ensure that your destiny will be that which will build you and not destroy you.

Chapter 6

Have you ever considered the importance of the mind and how vital a role it plays in your actions and your outlook?

Consider for just a moment that whatever you do in life from day to day, minute to minute, second to second, must first be conjured up in your mind. In other words, before you do anything, there must first be a thought that ultimately initiates it. The truth of this reality says to you that your thoughts are so very important to what you will be, what you will do and ultimately, what you will achieve in life.

From an insignificant gesture of scratching one's head, to a great feat of earning a doctorate degree from one of the country's most prestigious universities, neither could occur without an initiating thought. For this reason, we can ascertain that everything is triggered by a thought process. Acknowledging this gives credence and significance to the slogan adopted by the United

Negro College Fund, "A mind is a terrible thing to waste." How true a phrase this really is!

When I consider the multitude of inmates both male and female who have lost their freedom, I often wonder about the thoughts that led to their criminal actions. (Of course, I am only speaking of those who were justly convicted). How did the thought of committing illegal acts enter into their minds (certainly we are not born with criminal intents)?

Who planted the thought to break the law? Was it the company they were in? It could have been something they saw or just maybe it was something that they heard. The thought had to be planted and it triggered an action that led to their incarceration.

I would guess that many of these unfortunate individuals (if interviewed today) would caution each of you to be careful of the thoughts that you allow to enter and linger in your mind. As a matter of fact, *"What have you been thinking about lately?"* Have you had thoughts of optimism or thoughts of pessimism, thoughts of decency or thoughts of indecency, thoughts of good or thoughts of evil?

In the Bible, the Apostle Paul writes to us out of the book of Philippians 4:8 these words.

"Finally, brethren, whatsoever things are true, whatsoever things are honest, whatsoever things are just, whatsoever things are pure, whatsoever things are lovely, whatsoever things are of good report; if there be any virtue, and if there be any praise, think on these things ." Notice that the array of things that this great biblical personality instructs us to place our concentration on, are all positive. This would lead me to believe that there is great benefit in thinking on the positive as opposed to the negative.

For those who are incarcerated, just think of how different their life would be today if they had replaced those thoughts of evil with thoughts of love and honesty. Yes, your thoughts do trigger your actions and ultimately, your destiny. Therefore, you must pay close attention to what you allow to enter your mind. Guard your mind against the many cares of this world that often come camouflaged in innocence, but their end is often deception and destruction. After all, why use thoughts to your detriment when they could be used for your benefit. Thoughts are indeed this powerful!

If you subscribe to Theological Creativity, then you agree with me that, *"in the beginning God created the heavens and the earth."* Consider that God had no warehouse, factory or manufacturing plant in which He created all that exists today. There were no raw materials or cost of goods sold on hand for Him to consider. He simply brought the sun, moon, stars, waters, heaven, earth, mankind and all living things into existence with His spoken word. Psalm 33:6 affirms this belief as it says, *"By the word of the Lord were the heavens made; and all the host of them by the breath of his mouth."*

However, when we examine this theology more closely we understand Saint John 1:1, *"In the beginning was the Word, and the Word was with God, and the Word was God."* In the Greek, the Word is described as the *"logos"* or more plainly the *"thought."* So now, put it all together. When God created everything, He did so by His thought which afterwards He spoke with His voice. Therefore, if you are indeed created in the image of God and after His likeness, how much more can you bring about things by your thoughts, words and actions?

It is important to change your attitude and start thinking differently about yourself and your future. I am certain that there are people around you that try to plant negative thoughts in your mind about you and your destiny. Remember what God spoke to the prophet Jeremiah, *"For I know the thoughts that I think toward you, saith the Lord, thoughts of peace, and not of evil, to give you an expected end."* God desires that you reach a good and successful future.

There is a powerful quote by Frank Outlaw which says, *"Watch your Thoughts. They become your Words. Watch your Words. They become your Actions. Watch your Actions. They become your Habits. Watch your Habits. They become your Character. Watch your Character. It becomes your Destiny!"*

Let thoughts of love, honesty, purity, optimism and good, propel you toward a bright and promising future.

A Great Fruit Basket

The wonderful thing about a fruit basket is its diverse composition. Many things sweet and a few things tart, yet all things colorful and to the pallet absolutely wonderful.

Chapter 7

Now, for all vegetarians and fruit lovers, hold on just a moment. Before you conjure up thoughts of an assortment of delectable treats fresh from the garden, please know I am speaking of a different kind of fruit basket. The fruit that I wish for you to consider are not apples, oranges, grapes, pears and the like. There is one fruit described in the New Testament passage of Galatians.

The Apostle Paul writes to the people located in the city of Galatia these words: "...*the fruit of the Spirit is love, joy, peace, longsuffering, gentleness, goodness, faith, meekness, temperance...*". Why would Paul refer to these adjectives as fruit? Well, I believe that Paul is giving an analogy and speaking in figurative terms to a people concerning how they should handle and interact with others. After all, your actions and demeanor sometimes speak louder than your words.

Consider the turmoil that our world is in and the many conflicts, rages and acts of violence that we witness on a daily basis both here and abroad. It seems that Paul's suggestion of you being a person of godly fruit can make such a difference in this season and time. Imagine the entire world filled with the fruit of the Spirit. Wow! We would have no need for weapons, military, correctional facilities or penal institutions.

Okay, I'm visualizing someone asking, *"Can this become a reality?"* I suppose I did get a little carried away in thought. Realistically, there will always be a need for law enforcement, however if you and I decide to manifest the fruit of the Spirit, we will directly impact the amount of evil and negativity in the world!

You may question whether these qualities will really bring about change in our world today, as bad as things appear to be. Well, I believe that Paul was inspired by God to give the people of his day instructions and advice on living peaceful lives. When we allow the Spirit to be present in our lives, we will begin to see the nine characteristics mentioned in the book of Galatians! Let's examine each attribute individually.

Love

Needless to say, love is an awesome and powerful tool to offset evil. Love is so powerful that it can ignore and overcome offenses, injustices, faults and failures. As a matter of fact, love doesn't need companionship or agreement. I can love you regardless of what you may think or how you might feel about me. My love for someone does not necessitate them loving me. Now that's powerful!

Joy

This is very significant to your outlook on life. The joy Paul speaks of is an inner joy that extends well beyond an emotion experienced as the result of receiving a gift or good news. Everyday will not necessarily be a great day. If you focus on something good God has done for you, then even on that day you can still experience joy! In religious circles, we have this saying: *"Lord, give me a joy that this world cannot give and therefore this world cannot take away from me."* That's an inner joy!

Peace

I believe that Paul is referring to an inner peace similar to the joy just mentioned. Let's face reality! There seems to be an ongoing conflict in our world that may never end. Yet, you can pray to God for a peace (inner peace) that will pass all understanding and comprehension. I desire the peace of God that keeps me calm when chaos is visibly raging all around me.

Longsuffering

Consider all the impatience in our world today. People are seemly unwilling to tolerate anything from anyone. Our schools have become "no tolerance" educational facilities. Our criminal justice system says, *"Three strikes and you're out."* Society says once addicted, always addicted. It goes on and on. It just seems that everyone's patience is wearing thin. Even road rage is on the rise. We can't get what we want fast enough, and everyone is searching for instant answers and results.

Gentleness

I am learning the importance of a gentle spirit. There is something to be said of people who can handle serious and difficult matters with gentleness and sensitivity. Our world would be a much friendlier place if people were gentle, one with another.

Goodness

Must we expound on this characteristic of the Spirit? All of us can better this world and ourselves by practicing goodness. Make up your mind today to be an agent of good deeds. Do good works, speak kind words and watch the atmosphere around you immediately change for the better.

Faith

To exist in this world at all, you must have a level of faith in something. People of God believe faith to be absolutely essential to our relationship with God and our ability to receive and achieve anything in this world. It is your faith in God that pleases Him and allows Him to interact with you and on behalf of others. It is the substance of the things we hope for and the evidence of things promised to us, but not yet materialized.

Meekness

God honors a meek and humble spirit. Meek individuals recognize the reality of evil, but understand that only the divine mercy and favor of God averts horrific disaster and discomfort. They realize there is no existence apart from God.

Temperance

Temperance has value in one's life because it teaches us moderation. Moderation can always benefit you whether it pertains to your eating habits, or other enjoyments of life. Learning to avoid an excessive mentality can only help you to live a well-balanced life.

Now combine all of these Godly spiritual characteristics and make them part of your daily thoughts and actions. Remember, there is a spiritual fruit basket. Eaten daily, it can change your life, community and world. Have you dined on your spiritual meal today?

Become A Finisher

The valuable lesson that we all learned as children from the story of the Tortoise and the Hare, is that the race is not given to the swift, but victory goes to the one who completes the race.

Chapter 8

*S*omeone once said, *"It's not where you begin, but it is where you finish that matters."* I have often pondered what it is that keeps and prevents people from completing what they have begun. In our world, we are inundated with individuals who are constantly talking about doing things. Some have even begun various things, but have yet to complete them.

Sometimes people step out to accomplish things God did not commission. Please know that this results in an uphill battle that most often leads to dissatisfaction and incompletion. You must be sensitive to the voice of God speaking to you and the will of God for your life.

There are also times when people transfer from one thing to another. They begin various tasks, but never complete any of them. This type of individual is often referred to as a *"jack of all trades and master of none."* We recognize God's ability to create multi-talented people who consistently complete tasks. They possess a quality which speaks volumes of their successes.

Using Christ as our example, we see Jesus coming to earth as an infant, born to a virgin named Mary. He had a specific task to redeem mankind from the clutches and bondage of sin and death. John 3:16 says, *"For God so loved the world that he gave his only begotten Son, that whosoever believeth in him should not perish, but have everlasting life."* Although this mission is very specific, we witness Jesus Christ doing many other things during his 33½ year life span. He heals the sick and restores mental sanity to lunatics. He feeds the hungry and clothes the naked. He ministers in various synagogues, villages, cities – even remote areas such as deserts, wildernesses and mountain peaks. He even raises the dead from the grave.

From this example, we see that the many miracles and mighty benevolent acts of Jesus were beneficial to the receivers. Just ask the man born blind who received his sight at the benevolence of Christ. This man testifies today that, *"I once was blind, but now I see."* Ask the woman who suffered an embarrassing bleeding disorder for twelve long years. She speaks to us today that, *"the doctors took advantage of my condition by bleed-*

ing me of all the money I had, but one touch of Jesus' garment healed what doctors said could not be healed."

Consider this reality: with all the good Jesus did; had He not died on the cross of Calvary and rose again, all of His good accomplishments on planet earth would have been for naught. Consequently, He would be considered a failure today!

You and I should thank the Lord that Jesus Christ was a finisher. We can have an outlook of victory and not defeat, because Christ is a finisher. We can declare ourselves the head and not the tail, because He is a finisher. Today, you are above and not beneath, because our Lord and Savior is a finisher.

Now you must believe if this same power of Christ dwells in you, then you can be a finisher too! Stop allowing people to sow negative seeds into your life by claiming that you are inadequate for this challenge or that task. Paul says in Philippians 4:13, *"I can do all things through Christ which strengtheneth me."* Let this biblical truth become your rallying cry today!

There are a few vital points you must understand to become a finisher.

- First of all, know that what you set out to do is in the divine will of God. This is so very vital because if God is for you, then He is more than the entire world against you. Everyone wants to know that they are connected to the right resources that can assist their efforts.

- Secondly, you must wait on the proper time and season to begin what God has ordained or given you permission to do. Everything in life has a purpose and a season. A farmer can become very frustrated trying to grow fruit and vegetables out of season. Likewise, you will lose hope in completing a task if you are not attuned to its season.

- Thirdly, you must be committed to the task or tasks assigned to you. Be steadfast and unmovable in your efforts. Give it all that you have, knowing that the end shall be one of victory.

- Lastly, when the task is finished, give God the glory and watch Him not stop there. He will take you on to even greater tasks and greater victories.

Now, that you have the instructions to become a finisher, why not make the decision to be one! Decide to be an individual that looks back over life to see numerous tasks completed and goals accomplished! I believe that God gives to each of us assignments and tasks. Also, I firmly believe that He does not assign something to us without first determining whether we could complete the assignment. He will also provide resources necessary for its completion. When you understand all of this, the only thing left to consider is whether God is in the midst of your attempts.

Apostle Paul's words to the church at Philippi: *"Being confident of this very thing, that he which hath begun a good work in you will perform it until the day of Jesus Christ:"*

Confidence in God will help us finish everything that He allows us to start.

Thinking Outside Of The Box

ॐ

Anyone can operate within the confines of routine structure and be numbered with the vast majority of those who will settle for mediocrity. However, true brilliance is reserved for those who will dare visit possibilities beyond that which is considered the norm.

Chapter 9

Maintaining your relevance and reaching your purpose leads to your success in life.

I am a great student of history. I love to travel to wonderful sights around the world. I recently took a cruise of the Baltic Sea. I toured the various parts of the Baltic States and the former Russian Republics. I marveled at the history dating back thousands of years.

While strolling down cobble-stoned streets, praying in the various gothic churches, cruising the Baltic waterways and touring various castles, the knowledge imparted by our tour guides amazed me. Listening with my ears and visualizing with my eyes, I received a glimpse of ages past as I visited many of the ruins.

While touring Drottningholm Castle in Stockholm, Sweden, I was amazed to see what had been the norm for luxurious living in the twelfth and thirteenth centuries. When I compared that castle with the modern mansions of this twenty-first century, there really were no comparisons with regard to conveniences and accommodations. Many multiple staircases, lack of air-conditioning and forced heat would make those European castles unattractive and undesired. Today, we enjoy elevators, escalators, moving sidewalks, climate-controlled air and heat in our modern day estates!

While touring the Russian Orthodox Church and the oldest Lutheran church in Tallinn, Estonia, I saw old gothic buildings of great significance to the religious people of that era. Today they seem cold, lifeless, and museum-like. They are now tourist attractions rather than sanctuaries of worship and praise to God. We are now in a "mega-church" society where ministries have become *city like* with many conveniences to accommodate people from all walks of life.

One must ask the all-important question: *"Did these past attractions simply deteriorate, or did leadership fail to evolve in creative thought?"* Considering these sights, I could not help pondering, *"What will people think of my leadership one hundred years from now?"* Will my legacy continue to flourish upon a relevant foundation or will it slowly end as a result of subsequent leaders' inability to *"Think Out Of The Box"*?

I believe progression is now so rapid that before one area can be adequately perfected, someone has already begun the initiation of something better. Let's face one all-important fact: life is always evolving and things in life are always changing. In fact, the only thing you have to do to become outdated and useless is *nothing*!

Have you ever considered that in order for change to occur, someone must think differently than others? One must be able to see what others cannot see or, at least, dare to believe something that is beyond what is common and normal.

I appreciate the many inventors regardless of whether their areas of expertise are agriculture, science or other technologies and arenas in life. I am enjoying air travel, satellite television, the Worldwide Web, global banking, and even microwave ovens (well...every now and then when I'm in a rush). Yet, for you and I to enjoy these modern-day accommodations, someone somewhere first dared to think "out of the box". Secondly, a remnant of courageous individuals had to share ideas that were sometimes ridiculed or never given serious previous thought.

Dr. George Washington Carver, Whitney Young, Dr. Charles Drew, Madame C.J. Walker,

Henry Ford, The Wright Brothers, President John F. Kennedy, (who endeavored to put the first man on the moon), and numerous others were and are *"out of the box"* thinkers.

Now, may I ask you a question: *"What is holding you in the box?"* Could it be the laughter of others, maybe its low self-esteem, perhaps it's a shyness or maybe insecurity. I want to succeed in inspiring you to think beyond where you are. Shake off the spirit of complacency and know that God has much more in store for you. As a matter of fact, where you are now is not your destiny. You will never reach your goal if you are unable to think beyond yourself in the present.

God has placed in each of us potential and abundant creativity. The dismal reality is that most of us only use a tiny fraction of the intellect that God has endowed us with. We allow failure and misfortune to box us in. We allow society to box us in. We allow family and friends to box us in.

Thus, we become imprisoned in the shape and form that others would desire for us; instead of becoming expanded and unlimited in the awesomeness of a great God who formed us in His image and after His likeness. You must by all, and any means necessary, break out of that tiny box that is suffocating your dreams, goals, desires and aspirations. Become an *"out-of-the-box"* thinker and live a refreshing life of relevance, meaning and purpose!

Leave the secure confines of the normal and begin to explore roads that have not been traveled and thoughts that have yet to exist. Instead of always trotting down existing paths, why not seek out a new path and leave a trail of creativity and possibilities.

Life Is Bigger Than You Think

Life may not be fair but if you will pay attention to it, you are certain to learn the most valuable lessons ever. These lessons will teach you that life is much bigger and more complicated than you ever imagined.

Chapter 10

Do you see life expanding beyond what is visible right now? It really is much bigger than you think and God is in control of its eternity.

I have learned over the few decades of my life that *Life* itself is much bigger than I ever thought it was or could be. I can remember during my adolescence taking life for granted, because I thought it was something that I could grab by the tail and rule with my mere wishes and whims. How sadly mistaken I was!

Considering that during my years of living in a good home, being reared by two responsible parents who trained me in the right way, *life was a ball*, *a piece of cake*, and *there was nothing to it at all*. However, as I became more and more independent of my parents, life began to evolve into something that was much bigger than I could have ever imagined.

I am requested to teach seminars and minister sermons all across this country. I often admonish young people in my audience to take advantage of living in a good home. I tell them not to take this small phase of life for granted because life will get complex in a quick hurry. I refer to my parent's home as *"the magic house."* Not wishing to add any validity to the belief in black magic, but simply acknowledging that I had no appreciation for some responsibilities in life.

Thinking back on those days, I can remember placing notes on the refrigerator, breadbox, and food cupboard that we were out of milk, bread or maybe peanut butter. Meanwhile, the next day those items would magically appear in the proper place. I can even recall driving the family station wagon and after returning the car to our garage on empty, the next day out of nowhere the fuel tank was filled again. Now, of course, most of you are getting my point that there was a time in life that carried very little value, because, so many things were provided by good parents.

Today, however, I can testify that life to me is bigger than it's ever been. There is no magic house or car that I possess. There are no parents that care for my needs because now I am a grown man with personal responsibilities along with those to my own family (wife, children and ministry). While life carries now for me, a much different focus than when I was a child, it still intrigues me. I am confounded and baffled many times on how life can present one thing today and something totally the opposite tomorrow.

As a matter of fact, sometimes I don't know what life is going to bring next. I haven't a clue to what the next news report will convey; what message the next phone call will bring; or what the next physical examination will discover. My mom often reminds me of this saying, *"Life may not be fair, but if you pay attention, it will teach you a whole lot."*

I sum up this saying by acknowledging, *"Yes mom, you're absolutely right and life is also much bigger than you think."*

I caution people to see life as Christ sees it. The Bible teaches us to seek a life that is bigger than us, larger than this world and much broader than our comprehension. There are so many lessons in life to be learned of cheer as well as sorrow, abundance as well as lack, of both victory and defeat. I am striving each day to enjoy the life that Christ speaks about when he declares to

His disciples, *"I am come that you might have life and that you might have it more abundantly."*

There is a life that Christ wants us to enjoy in the spirit that will help us to maintain a healthy balance in the natural, even when things don't seem to be beneficial to us. After all, this is when we are most challenged in life. It is not the times of laughter, times of wholeness, times of strength and times of prosperity when we have issues, but it is the dark and dismal seasons that seem to never end that cause us sometimes to lose our faith and our way.

After finding that *"bigger"* life that our Savior speaks of, you may decide to reflect on why seeing the "big picture" was so difficult. You may then recognize that your initial focus was too narrow, limited and shortsighted, thus inhibiting the realization of your vision. Imagine basking in the wonderful shadow of a life that grants you great possibilities when others around you in similar situations are fainting, faltering and giving up! This is the realm of the spiritual life that all of us can experience, enjoy and be heirs to. The "eternal life" is one that far exceeds what we can ever comprehend through the limitations of our mere finite minds.

I encourage you to see life bigger than you can think. Stop allowing a bad day to shape your outlook and future. Don't allow the disappointments of a season to dispel your belief in a brighter day. There is much more to life than meets the eye. The realities of today neither handcuff God nor do they tie His hands so that He cannot work things out for our betterment.

As a matter of fact, for those of us who look to a bigger life and eternal life with God, it is St. Paul that reminds us that, *"All things work together for the good to them that love God; them who are the called according to His purpose."* This word ought to help you to see that things are not as bad as they may seem. Stop apologizing and saying that life has *"dealt you a bad hand,"* because the reality is this: our God is bigger than any hand that life deals you. Your life, spiritually and naturally, can become more abundantly blessed than you could ever have thought.

What Do You See?

Spiritual sight begins with a thought and a picture in your mind. Be careful with these visual seeds, for they determine the harvest of your life.

Chapter 11

What you are able to see can prove to be the difference between your success and your failure. What Do You See?

Seemingly, it's a very simple question, yet it has much more meaning than meets the natural eye (no pun intended). Our sight, regarded as one of our five senses, is so very powerful and advantageous to our life. Still, there are times when natural sight can prove to be detrimental to our success and productivity.

Saint Paul in biblical New Testament writings admonishes us to walk by faith, and not by sight. What a profound word that this revered apostle gives his readers and hearers. After all, it is without question that most individuals, if not all, would much rather control or navigate their lives in the light of day rather than in the darkness of night. As a result, Paul nonetheless makes a salient urging of us to do the opposite. Perhaps he was keenly aware of some of the dangers of placing too great an importance on the ability to naturally see.

So much is made for the case of sight. There is a very popular phrase from Missouri, the *show-me state* that says, *"Seeing is believing!"* This thought perpetuates the belief that only those things that can be visualized are certain and sure. If you subscribe to this belief, then I will assure you that you are limiting and alienating yourself from so many truths and possibilities. In fact, there is so much more that exists than that which meets the natural eye.

I firmly believe in the natural realm, which consists of the things that we know and understand, the things that we see and feel, and the things that are rational to the normal intellect. However, being a man of God with strong spiritual convictions, I also believe, unapologetically, in a spiritual realm.

For it is in the spiritual realm that God does His best work by confounding the wisest intellects with His awesomeness and omnipotence. As a matter of fact, I am certain that when comparing the natural to the spiritual, that it is the spiritual realm that far outweighs and overshadows that which is normal and rational every single time. Paul again records in 2nd Corinthians

4:18, *"While we look not at the things which are seen, but at the things which are not seen: for the things which are seen are temporal; but the things which are not seen are eternal."*

Paul declares this truth to all who will dare believe that there is so much more than what meets the natural eye. Also, to those few who will receive this biblical truth, there are endless possibilities and probabilities that can transform them into the most optimistic creatures on the face of this earth. Just imagine for a moment, being able to see things that the majority of society can never imagine exists. How many times have you needed a word or a vision of what God was doing at a very crucial time or season in your life?

In the Old Testament Book of 2nd Kings, we are reminded of what a godly and faithful person can see and how such spiritual sight can calm your fears during times of attack. The prophet Elisha and his servant Gahazi were encamped by the armed forces of the king of Syria. This military force was commissioned to do the man of God great harm. The Syrian army surrounded the prophet's tent. When they awakened, it was the servant, Gahazi, who warned the prophet Elisha that they were in great danger and that there was no way out.

The Bible declares that Elisha looked out of that same tent at the same situation and declared to his servant, *"Fear not: for they that be with us are more than they that be with them."* Elisha prayed for God to open the eyes of his servant (this was a spiritual request, for Gahazi was well endowed with natural sight). At the request of Elisha, Gahazi was able to see as his master saw, and he too now witnessed that surrounding the Syrian army was the Lord's hosts with horses and chariots of fire!

This biblical truth ought to encourage each of us to remember that there is a spiritual realm that is all-powerful and existing every second of every day. *"What do you see today?"* Will you continue to be confined to the short-sightedness of Gahazi or will you launch out into the chambers of spirituality that brought Elisha a great and awesome victory when the odds appeared to be stacked against him?

Most people will not be able to see beyond the bombardment of negative and pessimistic news that is so often prevalent. I challenge you to see through to the spirit:

• See God working things out for your good.

• See a light at the end of that dark tunnel.

- See a silver lining overwhelming every dark cloud.
- See God increasing your faith through sickness.
- See God supplying your needs through losing that job.
- See God teaching you patience in the midst of that tumultuous relationship.
- See your child or children obedient and successful.
- See yourself walking in a positive light.
- See yourself prosperous.
- See yourself as healed and delivered, the head and not the tail.
- See yourself as above and not beneath, a victor and not a victim.
- See yourself as an overcomer.
- See yourself as the lender and not the borrower.
- See yourself as a productive and progressive King's child.

Your spiritual vision will improve if you realign your sight beyond that which is natural to the realm of the supernatural.

The Value Of Time

❦

Those who have little respect for time will experience much of time passing them by. Time is so fleeting, that it will never be this time again.

Chapter 12

*T*ime can become valuable to you if you don't make excuses.

In the book of the preacher Ecclesiastes, we learn that *"To everything there is a season, and a time to every purpose under the heaven."* This anointed and wise sage conveys to us the following in the first eight verses of his third chapter. He says that there is *"A time to be born, and a time to die; a time to plant, and a time to pluck up that which is planted; A time to kill, and a time to heal; a time to break down, and a time to build up; A time to weep, and a time to laugh; a time to mourn, and a time to dance; A time to cast away stones, and a time to gather stones together; a time to embrace, and a time to refrain from embracing; A time to get, and a time to lose; a time to keep, and a time to cast away; A time to rend, and a time to sew; a time to keep silence, and a time to speak; A time to love, and a time to hate; a time of war, and a time of peace."*

One could only ascertain from this informative biblical passage that God operates according to His divine purpose within the seasons and times of life. He never does anything out of order or at a whim, but He carefully crafts, designs, and orchestrates at the appropriate times. This should cause us to continually seek an understanding of time and how it affects our success and destiny.

I have a disdain for people who do not value time; procrastinators, sluggards, and lazy folk. These persons will always come up short as it pertains to maximizing the life that God has ordained. How many people can you list who possess great potential and talents, but have no *get up and go?* I have known of many others with brilliant ideas, but always putting them off till tomorrow. Consider this! If God has carefully ordained a purpose for our lives, and if again, He operates by time, then we must have an appreciation for the value of His timing. Otherwise, we could miss our ordained purpose.

One of our major problems is the lack of respect that we give God when it comes to our lives. Sometimes it's very easy to declare ourselves totally independent of anyone including God. However, we must acknowledge God because it was God who formed mankind from the dust of the earth, and it is God who gives us life, health, and strength!

God speaks to the prophet Jeremiah these words, *"Before I formed thee in the belly I knew thee; and before thou camest forth out of the womb I sanctified thee, and I ordained thee a prophet unto the nations."* God expresses to His prophet that his conception was meaningful and with specific intent. Notice that God is not adapting to Jeremiah's life, but helping the man of God to understand he needs to submit to the will of God, because God's will is purposeful and subject to divine timing.

Jeremiah is not isolated with respect to the purposes and timing of God, but each and every one of us has been carefully and masterfully created by God for a specific purpose and calling. However, because God gives to each of us a free moral will and the ability to accept or reject that will, we can miss out on determining our purpose because we are not tuned in to the appropriate timing of His will for us.

Remember earlier I quoted the wise man in his discourse saying, there is *"a time to be born, and a time to die; a time to plant, and a time to pluck up that which is planted; A time to kill, and a time*

73

to heal; a time to break down, and a time to build up, etc." Now, consider that if we don't value time or have an appreciation of time, then we could be attempting to plant when it is actually time to harvest. Now tell me, is that not frustrating? Perhaps you're now recounting some of your failures and missteps in life. Could it be that you did not consider the time? Maybe you had a wonderful plan or idea, but the timing was wrong. Yet, maybe you were ordained for this purpose or that calling, but you missed your time.

I think you're getting my point that timing is not just meaningful, and purposeful, but timing is absolutely everything. It is an utmost and all important commodity in life. The proper timing (God's timing) is the difference between success and failure, fulfillment and disappointment, being effective or being non-effective, being efficient or simply a waste.

I have always had a great appreciation for time. Accordingly, I set goals and act hastily to maximize the time that God has given me while attempting to accomplish all that the Lord has ordained for my life. When you hear people make the statement, *"He doesn't let any grass grow under his feet,"* I promise you that they are referring to me. You see, it's not that I believe you always have to be doing something, because I am firmly persuaded that there is also a time to rest and stand still. My belief confirms to me that God has great things in store for me. I want to ensure that I don't miss my season because of my misuse of time.

I want to always respect time, and if you want to be successful in life, then you too must value time. Therefore, we must ask God for understanding of His will for our lives, his timing, and seasons for His will to be performed. At the end of the day, my point is as simple as this: If you were traveling by airplane to an important affair and you knew the plane departed at a certain time, you would make sure you didn't miss that flight, by arriving at the airport prior to the plane's departure time. Your failure to acknowledge or value that departure time would cause you to miss your flight and miss out on that important event. Without delay, organize yourself to maximize and value the time that God has given you.

The Bottom Line

To every beginning there is a conclusion and to be successful, one must carefully consider the costs of their ending before ever beginning.

Chapter 13

*F*ocus on that which is most important in life.

The 12th chapter of Ecclesiastes brings about a thought of conclusiveness that I believe every person on earth must consider and come to terms with. Verses 13 and 14 admonishes us accordingly, *"Let us hear the conclusion of the whole matter: Fear God, and keep his commandments: for this is the whole duty of man. For God shall bring every work into judgment, with every secret thing, whether it be good, or whether it be evil."*

This biblical account is believed to have been penned by King Solomon who was credited with being the wisest man to walk the face of this earth besides Jesus Christ himself. Solomon was given exceptional wisdom through his humble request to God for unprecedented understanding in dealing with the children of Israel. History tells us that God not only accommodated him with sagely wisdom, but he was also afforded tremendous riches, wealth and honor.

Can you imagine having everything you need or could ever desire and the wisdom to appropriate it all in the proper manner? For most people this would be a fairy tale, something one could only wish for, but for Solomon it was his reality and life. Through his godly wisdom and understanding, Solomon records this very sober and thought provoking truth. He says to us today, *"Hear the conclusion of the whole matter."* In other words, *"I'm going to sum of life for you quick, easy and in simple terms."*

In all honesty, we have all found out in life that sometimes it is very easy to be misguided or misdirected toward things which appear to be of utmost importance, only to discover later that they had very little merit or impact. Have you ever spent much of your valuable time chasing something only to realize that you were simply "chasing your tail" and making little or no progress?

Well, I have on many occasions majored in the minor things of life and vice versa. A fair question is, *"How can you know early on what has meaning and purpose in life?"* After all, what can you truly know without the experiences of trial and error?

Solomon tries to save us some headache, grief, pain and most of all wasted time, by simplifying things from his experiences of life. *"Hear the conclusion of the whole matter,"* he says to us. What is the bottom line O wise king of Israel? He says it is to *"Fear God and keep His commandments: for this is the whole duty of man."* Sounds quite simple, doesn't it? Well, in reality it really is pretty elementary.

He acknowledges that when it is all said and done, God is the only true judge that will demand for every action we take "an answer." He will have the complete and total record of our lives. We all must give an account. There will be no legal representative for us, and we will not be afforded the option of pleading the fifth.

Think about your life's status at this very moment. Reflect back on your past and consider what has motivated your actions. What has been the driving force in your life? Have you spent much of your time attempting to impress others? Have you even desired to perform the will of God and to do what is pleasing in His sight?

Beloved, take it from Solomon. This man clearly walked where few men have ever trod and lived a life that very few could even comprehend or fathom. When it came to riches, he was the wealthiest man on earth. In relative terms, his riches would dwarf that of Bill Gates, Warren Buffet and the Saudi Kings all combined. His home consisted of 300 wives, 700 concubines, and servants so plenteous until nothing in his charge was ever un-kept, undone or out of order.

Most men's egos would glory in this wealth and status of life; but not Solomon. He clearly understood that to whom much was given, much would be required. He enjoyed the favor of God upon his life with great fear, caution, restraint, and soberness. He clearly noted that God was the giver and at any time God could take it all away. For that reason Solomon continually acknowledged God as his source and sustainer.

I believe that the horrendous economy we are experiencing is causing many people today to ask the question, *What is the bottom line* for dedicated employees have given their lives to the workplace only to be terminated without warning or hope for their future? Others have stored up for retirement and leisure only to see their life savings evaporate in the smoke of fraud, embezzlement, dishonesty and corporate greed. These unfortunate souls are left to ponder where their

priorities were and how did they became so misguided and misled.

Well, allow me to help you to get back on
track with your thinking, prioritizing, and
actions. The time is now to seek God's will for
your life and to understand His purpose for your
future. Don't wait until life gravely disappoints
you. Don't even spend your time trying to please
people by jumping through unnecessary hoops
trying to meet their standards, only to be reject-
ed in the end.

You should make a decision to fulfill the commandments of God and to hear His voice in the
midst of your thoughts, desires and actions. Cut
to the chase and make God's will for your life,
your greatest priority and endeavor. It's okay to
gain some things here on planet earth, but even
more so, begin to *"Set your affection on things
above, and not on things on the earth."* It is important for you to consider the true bottom line in
this world of hustle and bustle.

The Certainty Of Change

There are very few guarantees in life; however one absolute guarantee is that everything in life will change.

Chapter 14

*T*here is a familiar song with lyrics that go something like this:

Everything must change, nothing stays the same,

Everyone must change, for nothing and no one goes unchanged,

The young become the old, and mysteries do unfold,

But that's the way of time, for everything must change...

Have you ever considered how true these lyrics and statements are? All one has to do is to look in the mirror on a daily basis and you are sure to notice the reality of the certainty of change. I guess what amazes me most in life is that although change is most certain, it often meets overwhelming resistance. I am sure that you noticed individuals who refused to update themselves or the things that they possess. The reason? They have simply grown comfortable and use to them.

It is often so easy for those on the outside looking in to give advice that will cause you to run into brick walls because of their inhibitions for change and lack of vision for you. People can become so *"status quo"* and comfortable doing the same thing the same way that suggestions of change are insulting to them. Well, I for one would like to discuss briefly the positive effects of change.

You see, God created each of us and everything that exists in this world with purpose and divine design to grow and to prosper, from the grass in the fields, to the creeping things of the dust, to the birds of the air, the fish of the sea, and most of all to you and me. We were all created for change and growth. The only way for us to reach our destiny and purpose is to evolve through various transformations and transitions. Anything that refuses to change and/or grow is destined to die.

You can never fulfill your purpose in life if you are not willing to be transformed. Think about it like this! The normal cycle of life is for an infant to become a child, for a child to reach adolescence, for an adolescent or teenager to mature into adulthood, and for adults to experience marriage, parenting and a retired life of relaxation and leisure. Now which of us would not subscribe earnestly to this fairytale scenario?

Yet, the reality of this life cycle example is that there is constant and consistent change throughout. I used to complain about getting older until an older person reminded me that the only alternative to getting older was to die. What a profound and sobering statement that a very wise patriarch made to me. I promise you that it has left such an indelible impression upon me that I have continued to repeat it and will continue to use it until the day I die.

Yes, change is evitable and certain. You can neither stop it nor detour it. O yes, there are many things that we can do and use to cover up change; but in the end, change always comes shining through whether we like it or not.

Consider that the cosmetic business is booming even in the midst of economic decline because many people try to overcome what they recognize as unwelcome change. There are even those who are still looking aimlessly for the *"fountain of youth."* These are those who are obsessed with the idea they will never age when in reality they have been aging all of their lives.

Let me admonish you to receive change as it comes. It is not your enemy, but rather it is the normality of life. God intended for us to change, to grow, to mature and to reach our destiny and purpose in Him. You might be in a wonderful place right now, but it is not where God is taking you. Know that God has more for you than what you are experiencing right now.

Never get so comfortable with where you are until you stop reaching for the next level. Never become so complacent with what you have that you become blind to what God is trying to give to you. Let the certainty of change propel you to that place in life that God has ordained for you. Always believe that there is another round in God for you and that NO ONE can stop you from reaching it.

Fighting change will only frustrate you with depression and a feeling of defeat. I encourage you to know that you are not defeated. Let the winds blow, the ups and downs of life pass, and the changes of life come. You can endure them, outlast them, and allow them to elevate you to your next level of success and victory.

You must begin to embrace change and to see it for what it is. Change is as normal as life itself, and if you will begin to pray God's will for your life, He will take you to a realm in Him. This is a realm where you can use change as a stepping stone to the next level as opposed to an unwelcome tenant. Know that change is certain and constant, and the sooner you accept it, the sooner you will begin your fulfillment of life. Embracing the certainty of change can help you to make the most of changes that are sure to come into your life.

The Art Of Forgiveness

One of the most challenging acts in life is to operate in a spirit of forgiveness. Failure to do so will only destroy humanity.

Chapter 15

*H*ave you ever considered the tremendous negative impact that a lack of forgiveness has on you? That's right, you heard me correctly. I did refer to a negativity that is sure to impact you and not the offender. Most people think that their refusal to forgive someone who has wronged them will handcuff that individual's ability to succeed in life. Well, if you think like this, you are sadly mistaken and misinformed. Your unwillingness to forgive will only hinder your dreams, aspirations and desires.

Can we be honest? Anytime there is an offense against us, it hurts. It sometimes demoralizes us, and it can even prove to be very damaging. These hurts most often occur when malicious intent is involved. Yet, even when the offense is unintentional, it can still be painful. No one ever wants to be embarrassed, walked on, or misused, yet these unpleasant happenings are enacted each and every day.

After all, none of us are perfect and this reality assures us that those simple, yet meaningful words *"I'm sorry"* will never be outdated or of non-effect. However, even amid the most unintentional offense, and despite the most sincere apology, there's still a human side that wishes to bunker down in unforgiveness.

In searching for wisdom and understanding when encountering offenses, we must turn to the word of God. Matthew 18:21-22 tells us that the disciple Peter came to Jesus and asked, *"Lord, how many times shall I forgive my brother when he sins against me, up to seven times?"* Jesus answered, *"I tell you, not seven times, but seventy times seven."* When you read the commentary of this particular text, you will find that Peter's inquiry was in consideration of one who offended him in one day.

This consideration would have us to believe that God leaves us no excuse when it comes to forgiving one another. Perhaps, the Lord knows something about forgiveness that we have yet to comprehend. Could it be that our ability to forgive others frees us to continue toward our destiny and purpose. It allows us to go forward without the excess baggage of emotional mood swings against someone who has wronged us?

Maybe the art of forgiveness is mandatory for us to prosper and to bask in the favor and blessings of God.

Whichever you subscribe to, I believe that forgiveness is absolutely necessary for us to remain healthy and mentally sound. I once taught a lesson entitled *"The Power of Your Thoughts."* I discussed how important it was to think positive thoughts and not allow pessimism to cloud your mind and brain waves. Negative energy will cause you to plummet into the dark dives of destruction and be unproductive and unhappy.

When you refuse to forgive others and to release your mind of resentfulness and hurt, you are only limiting your own potential and outlook on life. You then become consumed with some-one else's destruction until you are actually destroying yourself.

I know it's easier said than done when it comes to loving your enemy and doing good to those who maliciously offend you, but know that your good success is tied to your ability to forgive.

This is probably why I like to refer to forgiveness as an *"art."* It is not easy. Most times it's very difficult to wish someone well when they are unapologetically wishing evil toward you.

However, it is God's way and indeed *"God's way is always the best way. It is the right way."*

I encourage you to trust the words of Jesus in the Book of Matthew in the Bible, Chapter 8, and begin this day to practice the art of forgiveness. What really separates you from the crowd is when you refuse to harbor any ill thoughts toward your friends. By doing so, you will be among the few who have matured to a victorious place, having peaceful thoughts concerning those who despitefully misuse you.

A forgiving spirit will always win, because good will surely conquer evil every time. Know that life is certain to bring offenses, some small and many great, but also know that the power to forgive and move closer to your success is totally in your hands and control. Use your God-given power to eradicate the mindset of revenge, bad attitudes, holding grudges, channeling evil thoughts, and getting even.

Make a pledge to practice forgiveness each day, not only with your lips, but also in your actions. See forgiveness as a necessary principle to reach your God-ordained purpose and destiny. Don't fall into the devil's trap of an eye for an eye and a tooth for a tooth. That will only leave our society "blind" and unable to "chew".

See yourself living in an atmosphere free from malicious intents and vengeful thoughts toward anyone. Enjoy a mindset free from negativity and ill will. See forgiveness as your key toward a life of joy, peace and happiness. Only allow positive thoughts to linger in your mind and wish the best for everyone. Remember that the word of God says in Galatians 6:7, *"Be not deceived; God is not mocked: for whatsoever a man soweth, that shall he also reap."* Sow forgiveness and watch it come back to you. When offense comes your way, be strong enough to say *"I forgive you."*

The Power Of A Song

Music is a powerful force in our world that is used to influence the souls of mankind. What kind of pied piper are you?

Chapter 16

Years ago, one of Detroit's most famous radio personalities, Martha Jean *"the Queen"* Steinberg, would begin her noon radio program with music by the beloved Grammy Award winning singer and composer, the Reverend James Cleveland. The musical piece was entitled *"Without A Song"* and the lyrics went something like this:

Without a song the day would never end
Without a song the road would never bend
When things go wrong
A man hasn't got a friend unless God gives him a song

These lyrics would soothe thousands of people each and every day; because it is so true of how music and something as simple as a song can influence you. Music can get into your soul so much until it will cause you to move your body, pat your feet, and beat upon a table top with your fingers. There are melodies and lyrics that will even linger in your mind and thoughts long after the song have ended.

How many people have heard a song during the course of a day that was so touching until they hummed it even into the midnight hours, well after their normal sleep time? This is what we call the power of a song. Songs can even cause infants to move and bounce and we know that babies can't comprehend melodies and lyrics. Again, it's the power of a song!

I have learned to appreciate good music, because it can cause your day to breeze through faster than you realize. It can even create a pleasant atmosphere during periods of stress and pressure. A good song at the right time can ease tension. As a matter of fact, one aged thought even says that music *will calm the savage beast.*

Songs and music have become so powerful in this day and time until it is now a billion dollar industry. It is even possible for a songwriter to pen one *"hit"* that can catapult him or her into financial security for up to three generations. Now that's powerful!

Referring back to the lyrics of the song by the late Reverend James Cleveland, have you ever considered what this world would be like without a song? As I imagine and contemplate this thought adjectives such as dull, lifeless, bland, and boring immediately come to mind.

After all, it is songs that carry us through each and every day. It is those wonderful lyrics that cause us to smile in the midst of rough times. I can't count the number of times that I have attended or participated in funeral services where a song transformed an atmosphere of sorrow and mourning into joy.

It is without a doubt that this example, if none other, truly demonstrates the power of a song. A song can turn a frown upside down into a smile. A song can ease the burden of misery and pain. Think about what a song can do for you. The right song can brighten your darkest hour and shine a light into the midst of your nighttime.

Songs were a powerful tool that God gave His people the Israelites. They had Levites and worship leaders that could usher in the presence of the Lord with a song of praise and worship. Songs would lead them into battle, and carry them through victoriously. Their ability to sing brought great power to them, and was a threat to their enemies. Yet, we see God chastising them through Babylonian oppression, and when Israel was lead away into captivity, the Babylonians made fun of them and ridiculed them in their state of bondage. Suffering punishment at the will of God made them feel embarrassed, demoralized and defeated.

Their taskmasters required them to sing a song for their captors' cruel entertainment. God's people responded, *"How can we sing the Lord's song in a strange land?"* They would not sing and in captivity they hung their harps up in the willow trees and retired all of their musical instrumentation. Because they had been taken captive away from Jerusalem, they lost all motivation, will, inspiration, encouragement and desire. They sat by the rivers a defeated people with nothing to live for.

Yet, I say to you today that Israel had much to live for. Even in the midst of bondage, they still had life. Though their present state was depressing, their future was still ahead of them, and able to be shaped into whatever they desired it to be. They forgot that source of power that the enemy could not take away. Yes, it was their ability to sing. For you see, it was their singing that would usher in the presence of God. O yes! The enemy wanted them to sing for entertainment, but they should have *"turned the tide"* on the enemy by singing and appealing to the grace of a merciful

God. If they had understood the power of a song, they probably would have ended their captivity much sooner.

Let this inspirational message teach us concerning the value and power of a song. Without a song, I believe the day would never end. Without a song, the road would never bend. Yes, when things go wrong, a man hasn't got a friend unless God gives him a song. Never underestimate the power of a song.

About
Charles H. Ellis III

Charles H. Ellis III is the Senior Pastor of Greater Grace Temple in Detroit, Michigan. He pastors nearly 8,000 and is known as a leader *"with a heart for people."* In 1996 after succeeding his father, David L. Ellis, he and the ministry have continued to forge ahead with God's favor, bringing into fruition a new 36-million dollar worship facility. This state of the art masterpiece includes a 4,000-seat auditorium, an elegant 600-seat banquet hall and conference center.

Under his leadership Greater Grace Temple now has nearly 250 compartmental ministries including the following, which extend beyond its religious mandate:

- Over 100 Housing Units for seniors and families
- Two Charter Schools (Grades K- 8)
- Montessori Day Care Center
- Fully Operational Bookstore

- Multipurpose Activity Center
- 18-Hole New Rogell Golf Course
- Print Shop
- Television and Recording Studios
- Travel Agency
- Funeral Home

Most of these outreaches are headquartered at the church's 140-acre complex known as the *"City of David."* These humanitarian outreaches positively impact the Detroit community where he is a respected leader. Here are some of his honors and board appointments:

- Board member of the Vanguard/DMC Hospital Group
- Board member of the Detroit Zoological Society
- Board member of the Metropolitan Detroit YMCA
- Chairman, Mayor's Strategic Task Force (Detroit Works Project)
- Chairman, Detroit Tigers Baseball Negro League Celebration
- Founder & President of The Master's Commission
- Founder & President of the GGT Non-profit Housing Corporation

Charles H. Ellis III serves as the Presiding Prelate of the Pentecostal Assemblies of the World, Inc. Through television and radio mediums, Bishop Ellis brings the message of God's love to a potential 50 million viewers on *"The Word Network"* and other television and broadcast outlets.

Bishop Ellis is a Business Administration graduate of Wayne State University with a major in Accounting. He also holds an honorary doctorate from Aenon Bible College and has been a guest lecturer on various occasions at the Harvard School of Divinity.

Notes

Notes

Notes